THE INTENTIONAL YEAR JOURNAL

a guided journey into freedom, peace, and purpose

HOLLY + GLENN PACKIAM

NavPress

A NavPress resource published in alliance
with Tyndale House Publishers

NavPress is the publishing ministry of The Navigators, an international Christian organization and leader in personal spiritual development. NavPress is committed to helping people grow spiritually and enjoy lives of meaning and hope through personal and group resources that are biblically rooted, culturally relevant, and highly practical.

For more information, visit NavPress.com.

The Intentional Year Journal: A Guided Journey into Freedom, Peace, and Purpose

Copyright © 2023 by Glenn Packiam and Holly Packiam. All rights reserved.

A NavPress resource published in alliance with Tyndale House Publishers

NavPress and the NavPress logo are registered trademarks of NavPress, The Navigators, Colorado Springs, CO. *Tyndale* is a registered trademark of Tyndale House Ministries. Absence of ® in connection with marks of NavPress or other parties does not indicate an absence of registration of those marks.

The Team:
David Zimmerman, Publisher; Caitlyn Carlson, Acquisitions Editor; Elizabeth Schroll, Copy Editor; Olivia Eldredge, Operations Manager; Julie Chen, Designer; Sarah K. Johnson, Proofreading Coordinator

Cover illustration of color grid by Julie Chen. Copyright © 2022 by Tyndale House Ministries. All rights reserved.

Published in association with The Bindery Agency, www.TheBinderyAgency.com

All Scripture quotations, unless otherwise indicated, are taken from the Common English Bible, copyright 2011. Used by permission. Scripture quotations marked *MSG* are taken from *The Message*, copyright © 1993, 2002, 2018 by Eugene H. Peterson. Used by permission of NavPress. All rights reserved. Represented by Tyndale House Publishers. All rights reserved. Scripture quotations marked NIV are taken from the Holy Bible, *New International Version,*® *NIV.*® Copyright © 1973, 1978, 1984, 2011 by Biblica, Inc.® Used by permission. All rights reserved worldwide.

Some of the anecdotal illustrations in this book are true to life and are included with the permission of the persons involved. All other illustrations are composites of real situations, and any resemblance to people living or dead is purely coincidental.

For information about special discounts for bulk purchases, please contact Tyndale House Publishers at csresponse@tyndale.com, or call 1-855-277-9400.

ISBN 978-1-64158-656-6

Printed in China

29	28	27	26	25	24	23
7	6	5	4	3	2	1

CONTENTS

INTRODUCTION

God is the one who enables you both to want
and to actually live out his good purposes.

Philippians 2:13

Life tends to happen *to* us. The alarm goes off, and we stumble out of bed and begin our day, moving from one appointment to the next, mindlessly scrolling social media during the lulls between things. By the time we get home, our brains are fried and our souls are depleted, but our bodies just keep moving on autopilot. Prepare dinner, clean up the kitchen, take the dog for a walk, get the kids to bed, scroll social media again.

We don't have time to step back from our days, much less

from our lives, to examine what we're doing and why, right? Or so we think.

The frantic pace we find ourselves struggling to keep doesn't have to be our reality. We can live with a sense of vision, purpose, and deliberateness that helps us order our days. We can choose to interrupt the cycle of default living by *stopping intentionally* to examine *how* we want to live. By purposefully carving out time every year, we can pay attention to what God is doing in our lives and look ahead to where we are going.

This journal acts as a companion to your journey through *The Intentional Year*, guiding you through a rhythm of reflection and intention for the season ahead. In these pages, you'll process and engage with the five spheres of life outlined in *The Intentional Year* and cast a vision for purposeful living right where you are.

We recommend taking time away from the busyness of your daily life—whether it's a single day or a weekend—to give attention to the state of your soul and the pace of your life. For a dozen years or so, we (Glenn and Holly) have been carving out time for an annual retreat at the end of December or the beginning of January. Our retreat plan has ebbed and flowed during this time, but in recent years we've come up with a rhythm to guide us into a more intentional life. Here's what our retreat rhythm usually looks like:

- **Connect, share, and process:** For the first night of our retreat, we enjoy an evening out just to catch our breath and share our hearts with each other. Processing helps us shift our focus to rest and reflection from the chaos of normal life, with carpool driving, meal prep, work, parties—you get the idea. If you're single, an evening out might include treating yourself to an amazing meal or going to one of your favorite spots. It could also be fun to invite two or three trusted friends to join you on a retreat.

- **Reflect on the past and on what lies ahead:** The next morning, we each find a private spot to journal and pray reflectively about the previous year (or six months if we do this twice a year). We look back at the goodness of God and name the grief and gifts of the past season. Then we take time to look ahead and listen for God's direction. Is there a key word or theme we need to pay attention to, a sort of framing story for the season to come?

- **Connect, share, and process:** After a time of individual reflection and listening to God, we come together over lunch and process what God has shown us. We share from our journals and talk about any key words or themes we received from God regarding the months ahead.

- **Take an inventory of five spheres of life:** We spend the rest of the afternoon reflecting on the spheres of *prayer, rest, renewal, relationships,* and *work* and the rhythms that have characterized our lives in each of these spheres over the past year. What rhythms have helped us connect with God, stop and reflect, rest and renew? Which rhythms do we want to continue in the coming year? Are there any new practices we could start? What relationships have we invested in over the past year? Are there people we want to bring in close in the coming months, or relationships we need to let go of for a time? Finally, we evaluate the work we're doing—paid or unpaid—and ask the Lord to help us see if anything needs to change. Maybe the work doesn't align with the gifts God has given us, the growth we've experienced, or the capacity we actually have in this season.

- **Connect, share, and process:** Over dinner that evening, we discuss our inventory of practices, comparing notes and finding places of unity. Sharing and processing helps us shape a vision for the coming year.

- **Establish rhythms for the next season:** The final morning, we bring together everything we've been talking about and establish rhythms for each sphere of life in the coming year. What specific practices do we want to engage in that will help us pray, rest, be renewed, connect in relationships, and work?

- **Make a plan of action:** After a break for lunch, we do the unglamourous but crucial work of turning our list of practices for the next season of our lives into dates and times on the calendar. When will we go on dates? When will we set aside time for rest and renewal? When will we pray or work out or have friends over? If the practices we've established don't make it onto our calendar and become scheduled events, they will remain abstract ideas.

This rhythm for our annual retreats has anchored our marriage and household for more than a decade. It has become our garden box for fruitfulness, the trellis for our life on the vine.

Even if you don't start off a new season with an annual retreat, incorporating key practices at different points during the year can be a game changer. We pray that this journal will help you on your way to freedom, peace, and purpose in your spiritual life, practices of rest and renewal, relationships, and work.

part one

REFLECTION

There's a season for everything

and a time for every matter under the heavens:

a time for giving birth and a time for dying,

a time for planting and a time for uprooting what was planted,

a time for killing and a time for healing,

a time for tearing down and a time for building up,

a time for crying and a time for laughing,

a time for mourning and a time for dancing,

a time for throwing stones and a time for gathering stones,

a time for embracing and a time for avoiding embraces,

a time for searching and a time for losing,

a time for keeping and a time for throwing away,

a time for tearing and a time for repairing,

a time for keeping silent and a time for speaking,

a time for loving and a time for hating,

a time for war and a time for peace.

Ecclesiastes 3:1-8

LOOKING BACK

REVIEW

How are you feeling physically? What emotions are you aware of? Are you feeling happy, sad, angry, anxious? Write down what you observe.

_____

_____

_____

_____

_____

_____

_____

_____

_____

_____

_____

_____

_____

_____

_____

_____

_____

_____

_____

_____

_____

_____

What significant things happened over the past year?
Reflect on your thought processes, your conversations,
your actions. This might seem like a huge task, but just
write whatever comes to mind.

_____

_____

_____

_____

_____

_____

_____

_____

_____

_____

_____

_____

_____

_____

As you reflect on the past year, prayerfully ask God to bring things to mind. Ask him to show you where you've fallen short of his plan for your life. Ask him to make you aware of where or how you gave and received love or failed to do so. Ask, *What good could I have brought to someone but chose not to?*

_____

_____

_____

_____

_____

_____

_____

_____

_____

_____

_____

_____

_____

What were some of the high points, or mountaintops, over the past year?

_____

_____

_____

_____

_____

_____

_____

_____

_____

_____

_____

_____

_____

_____

What were some of the low moments, or valleys?

_____

_____

_____

_____

_____

_____

_____

_____

_____

_____

_____

_____

_____

_____

_____

_____

_____

What was an average day like? How did you feel in the morning and evening?

_____

_____

_____

_____

_____

_____

_____

_____

_____

_____

_____

_____

_____

_____

_____

_____

What issues or problems, if any, did you struggle with this year? What recurring problems, tensions, or struggles did you experience?

_____

_____

_____

_____

_____

_____

_____

_____

_____

_____

_____

_____

_____

_____

_____

Where did you discover gifts of joy over the past year?

_____

_____

_____

_____

_____

_____

_____

_____

_____

_____

_____

_____

_____

_____

_____

_____

Where did you experience sorrow and grief?

_____

_____

_____

_____

_____

_____

_____

_____

_____

_____

_____

_____

_____

_____

_____

_____

Where or how did you give and receive love?

_____

_____

_____

_____

_____

_____

_____

_____

_____

_____

_____

_____

_____

_____

_____

REJOICE

Reflect on the year month by month. What seemingly small things are you grateful for as you think about January, February, March, and so on? What are you grateful for that had a significant impact on you this year? Write down anything that comes to mind. Thank God for the gift of his presence throughout the year, for blessings, for the gift of relationships, for the ability and opportunity to give and receive love.

_____

_____

_____

_____

_____

_____

_____

_____

_____

_____

_____

_____

_____

REPENT

Reflect on where you have fallen short this past year. As you do, repent and ask for forgiveness for the ways you did not cooperate with the Holy Spirit and failed to give and receive love. Know that as you do, God meets you with grace, boundless love, and restoration. Ask the Lord to show you how to distinguish his voice of grace from your own voice of self-condemnation.

We have not loved you with our whole heart;

we have not loved our neighbors as ourselves.

We are truly sorry and we humbly repent.[1]

The Book of Common Prayer

How have you not loved God with your whole heart this year?

_____

_____

_____

_____

_____

_____

_____

_____

_____

_____

_____

_____

REQUEST

Ask the Lord for the grace to grow and participate in the Holy Spirit's work. Where do you sense the Holy Spirit leading you to grow this year?

_____

_____

_____

_____

_____

_____

_____

_____

_____

_____

_____

The best part of the gospel is that

God always meets us with grace.[2]

LOOKING FORWARD

Have you ever sensed the voice of God? When has it been clear? When have you struggled to know?

_____

_____

_____

_____

_____

_____

_____

Think for a moment about the season you've just been through. Are there any themes or patterns you observe?

_____

_____

_____

_____

_____

_____

_____

_____

_____

_____

_____

_____

_____

_____

_____

What might be some of the lessons the Lord has been trying to teach you? In which areas do you sense God inviting you to grow?

Think of a time when friends and family helped you discern the voice of God. What lessons can you take away from that experience?

_____

_____

_____

_____

_____

_____

_____

_____

_____

_____

_____

_____

_____

_____

_____

_____

TAKE THE POSTURE OF THE SERVANT

Pray the words that Moses, Abraham, Isaiah, and others prayed: "Here I am."

What area of your life would you rather God not disrupt?

_____

_____

_____

_____

_____

_____

_____

_____

_____

_____

_____

_____

_____

_____

Is there something you are holding on to and don't want
to surrender to the Lord?

_____

_____

_____

_____

_____

_____

_____

_____

_____

_____

_____

_____

_____

_____

_____

What is God asking you to say yes to?

_____

_____

_____

_____

_____

_____

_____

_____

_____

_____

_____

_____

_____

_____

_____

_____

What is God asking you to say no to?

_____

_____

_____

_____

_____

_____

_____

_____

_____

_____

_____

_____

_____

_____

_____

_____

_____

START WITH WHAT SCRIPTURE
HAS ALREADY REVEALED

How is God at work in the world? Think of the big arc of
the narrative of the Bible.

_____

_____

_____

_____

_____

_____

_____

_____

_____

_____

_____

_____

_____

_____

God's mission and character are revealed in Jesus. Which aspects of the life and ministry of Jesus stand out to you in this season?

_____

_____

_____

_____

_____

_____

_____

_____

_____

_____

_____

_____

_____

_____

_____

What are some of the things God calls all Christians to do?
Write down any specific texts that come to mind.

_____

_____

_____

_____

_____

_____

_____

_____

_____

_____

_____

_____

_____

_____

_____

LISTEN FOR THE CLEAR AND QUIET

What words and phrases are rising to the surface of your heart?

_____

_____

_____

_____

_____

_____

_____

_____

_____

_____

_____

_____

_____

What prayer is flowing out of you as you listen for God's voice?

_____

_____

_____

_____

_____

_____

_____

_____

_____

_____

_____

_____

_____

_____

Imagine yourself with Jesus. What is he saying to you about this season?

_____

_____

_____

_____

_____

_____

_____

_____

_____

_____

_____

_____

_____

_____

_____

If God has solidified a specific word or theme for the season ahead, write it here:

_____

_____

_____

_____

_____

_____

_____

_____

_____

_____

Every season has *limitations* and *invitations*.

There are things God is asking us to say no to

and things he is inviting us to say yes to.[3]

part two

INVENTORY

Search me, God, and know my heart;

test me and know my anxious thoughts.

See if there is any offensive way in me,

and lead me in the way everlasting.

Psalm 139:23-24, NIV

PRAYER

Jot down the way you pray. Is it spontaneous or scheduled? Do you sit and listen or walk and talk? Which prayer practice do you default to?

_____

_____

_____

_____

_____

_____

Prayer often resembles human connection. Consider what helps you connect with other people. Is the connection more cognitive or emotional? What makes you feel loved? What prayer practices most resemble that type of connection?

_____

_____

_____

_____

_____

_____

_____

_____

_____

_____

_____

_____

_____

_____

_____

Think about getting up tomorrow morning to engage in prayer in your default mode. Do you dread it or look forward to it? Sometimes discipline and diligence are the answer; other times, evoking delight is necessary.

_____

_____

_____

_____

_____

_____

_____

_____

_____

_____

_____

_____

_____

Consider testing out a new prayer practice (like psalm
praying, P-R-A-Y, silence, or *lectio divina*) for a short time.
For the next few weeks, only pray in that way. What effect
does it have on your life with God?

_____

_____

_____

_____

_____

_____

_____

_____

_____

_____

_____

_____

_____

_____

_____

This week, choose one or two prayer practices and keep a simple log of your observations as you engage in each practice. Paying attention to how you pray today will help you be more intentional about prayer tomorrow.

_____

_____

_____

_____

_____

_____

_____

_____

_____

_____

Prayer isn't simply one sphere of life, or one category or compartment. It is foundational to life.[4]

REST

SABBATH ACTIVITIES TO DO

What activities are life-giving to you?

_____

_____

_____

_____

_____

_____

_____

What helps you connect with the Lord?

_____

_____

_____

_____

_____

_____

_____

_____

_____

_____

_____

_____

_____

_____

_____

_____

What brings you rest?

_____

_____

_____

_____

_____

_____

_____

_____

_____

_____

_____

_____

_____

_____

_____

_____

What brings you delight?

_____

_____

_____

_____

_____

_____

_____

_____

_____

_____

_____

_____

_____

_____

_____

_____

SABBATH ACTIVITIES TO CEASE

What activities drain you?

_____

_____

_____

_____

_____

_____

_____

_____

_____

_____

_____

_____

_____

_____

_____

What distracts you from your family?

_____

_____

_____

_____

_____

_____

_____

_____

_____

_____

_____

_____

_____

_____

_____

_____

What disconnects you from the Lord?

SABBATH PLANNING

When will you set aside a day for Sabbath?

_____

_____

_____

_____

_____

_____

_____

_____

_____

_____

_____

_____

_____

_____

_____

What will you do?

_____

_____

_____

_____

_____

_____

_____

_____

_____

_____

_____

_____

_____

_____

_____

_____

What will you cease from doing?

_____

_____

_____

_____

_____

_____

_____

_____

_____

_____

_____

_____

We rest because God rested, and

we rest because we are free.[5]

RENEWAL

MENTAL AND PHYSICAL HEALTH

What physical exercise could you do consistently? How much time could you realistically devote to exercise in a week? (Even five minutes a day can help you feel better!)

_____

_____

_____

_____

_____

What nutritional changes would help you care better for your body? (For example, drinking more water, eating more vegetables and less sugar, taking more supplements.)

_____

_____

_____

_____

_____

_____

_____

_____

_____

_____

_____

_____

_____

_____

What types of activities help you stay in a good mental state? Could you schedule time even once a quarter to meet with a counselor or spiritual director who can help you pay attention to your soul?

_____

_____

_____

_____

_____

_____

_____

_____

_____

_____

_____

_____

_____

_____

What habits do you need to curb or stop so your life has more balance? (For example, cutting back on your consumption of social media or Netflix or alcohol.)

_____

_____

_____

_____

_____

_____

_____

_____

_____

_____

_____

_____

_____

_____

_____

Where can you work in more play or recreation?

How can care for your physical and mental health become more life-giving and fun?

_____

_____

_____

_____

_____

_____

_____

_____

_____

_____

_____

_____

_____

_____

READING

What themes or topics has God brought to mind as possible focuses for the season ahead?

_____

_____

_____

_____

_____

_____

_____

_____

_____

_____

_____

_____

_____

_____

_____

What do you typically read? Articles? Fiction? Nonfiction? What are some ways you can branch out and diversify your reading experience?

_____

_____

_____

_____

_____

_____

_____

_____

_____

_____

_____

_____

_____

_____

_____

_____

GRATITUDE

What are some tangible ways you can integrate regular practices of gratitude for . . .

. . . the basic provisions of life?

_____

_____

_____

_____

_____

_____

_____

_____

_____

_____

_____

_____

. . . moments of joy and simplicity?

. . . the people who have influenced your life in a positive way?

_____

_____

_____

_____

_____

_____

_____

_____

_____

_____

_____

_____

_____

_____

. . . memories with family and friends?

_____

_____

_____

_____

_____

_____

_____

_____

_____

_____

_____

_____

_____

_____

_____

_____

. . . the Lord's presence and work in your daily life?

_____

_____

_____

_____

_____

_____

_____

_____

_____

_____

_____

**Being intentional about renewing ourselves
physically, mentally, and emotionally is
essential. It's difficult to be intentional
about anything else if we—our bodies,
minds, emotions, and more—
are deteriorating and diminishing.**[6]

RELATIONSHIPS

What is the Lord inviting you to say yes to in your relationships this season?

_____

_____

_____

_____

_____

_____

_____

_____

_____

_____

_____

_____

_____

_____

_____

_____

_____

_____

_____

_____

_____

_____

_____

_____

_____

_____

In your relationships, what are you holding before the Lord with anxiety or fear right now?

_____

_____

_____

_____

_____

_____

_____

_____

_____

_____

_____

_____

_____

_____

_____

22222222

What is God asking you to let go of in your relationships?

What do you sense standing between you and healthy
relationships?

_____

_____

_____

_____

_____

_____

_____

_____

_____

_____

_____

_____

_____

_____

_____

SELF-AWARENESS

Where do you need to grow in self-awareness in your relationships? What tools could help you get there?

EMPATHY

Where do you need to grow in empathy in your relationships?

_____

_____

_____

_____

_____

_____

_____

_____

_____

_____

_____

_____

_____

_____

How can you better cultivate curiosity about others?

_____

_____

_____

_____

_____

_____

_____

_____

_____

_____

_____

_____

_____

_____

_____

_____

_____

DIFFERENTIATION

On a scale of 1 to 10 (1 being least true, 10 being most true), indicate your capacity for differentiation in relationships:

I remain myself as I move toward another person to understand their perspective and emotions.

1   2   3   4   5   6   7   8   9   10

I allow another person's experience of a situation to move me but not diminish my own experience of that situation.

1   2   3   4   5   6   7   8   9   10

I allow myself to think or feel differently about things than the people I'm close to.

1   2   3   4   5   6   7   8   9   10

CIRCLES OF RELATIONSHIP

Consider the relationships in your life. Where does each fall among the circles of relationship?

Family

_____

_____

_____

_____

Extended Family/Close Friends

_____

_____

_____

_____

_____

_____

_____

_____

_____

_____

_____

_____

_____

_____

_____

_____

_____

Colleagues/Friends

Acquaintances

_____

_____

_____

_____

_____

_____

_____

_____

_____

_____

_____

_____

_____

_____

_____

_____

_____

What are ways you connect with the people in your life?

_____

_____

_____

_____

_____

_____

_____

_____

_____

_____

_____

_____

_____

_____

_____

What are ways you want to grow in connecting with the people in your life?

_____

_____

_____

_____

_____

_____

_____

_____

_____

_____

_____

_____

_____

_____

_____

LEAN IN, LET LIE, LET GO

Who helps you pay attention to God's work in your life?

_____

_____

_____

_____

Which friends walk with you, challenge you, and
encourage you? How can you make more room for them?

_____

_____

_____

_____

_____

_____

_____

_____

_____

How can you become a better friend or bridge the gap
between you and someone you want a closer relationship
with?

_____

_____

_____

_____

_____

_____

_____

_____

_____

_____

_____

_____

_____

_____

_____

_____

Which relationships do you need to let go of or pull away from?

_____

_____

_____

_____

_____

Which relationships do you need to let lie for a season?

_____

_____

_____

_____

Which relationships do you sense the Lord prompting you to lean into this year?

_____

_____

_____

_____

What would it take to lean into these relationships?

**Relationships not only reveal our need for
the fruit of the Spirit, but they also become
an essential part of the ecosystem in
which his fruit grows in our lives.**[7]

WORK

How do you think about work? Is it more of a necessary evil or pain, or is it a holy call to join God in cultivating his world?

_____

_____

_____

_____

_____

_____

What drew you to the work you do? Regardless of
whether it is paid or unpaid, what is the burden you felt
or perhaps still feel when you think deeply about it? How
would you describe your burden in your own words?

_____

_____

_____

_____

_____

_____

_____

_____

_____

_____

_____

_____

_____

_____

Think of how you feel about work at your best moments.
What about it brings you joy?

_____

_____

_____

_____

_____

_____

_____

_____

_____

_____

_____

_____

_____

_____

_____

How does your work reflect these three elements: God's glory, the world's good, and your joy? Which elements, if any, are missing?

_____

_____

_____

_____

_____

_____

_____

_____

_____

_____

_____

_____

_____

How might God be inviting you to do your work well? In what areas have you been less than faithful in carrying out the work God has entrusted you with? Remember that we can freely confess our failures with honesty because God is abounding in mercy.

_____

_____

_____

_____

_____

_____

_____

_____

_____

_____

_____

_____

_____

_____

_____

PRAYER FOR VOCATION IN DAILY WORK

Almighty God our heavenly Father, you declare your glory and show forth your handiwork in the heavens and in the earth: Deliver us in our various occupations from the service of self alone, that we may do the work you give us to do in truth and beauty and for the common good; for the sake of him who came among us as one who serves, your Son Jesus Christ our Lord, who lives and reigns with you and the Holy Spirit, one God, for ever and ever. Amen.[8]

The way we work and the way we think about work have deep implications for our spiritual lives.[9]

part three

ACTION

"Walk with me and work with me—watch how I do it. Learn the unforced rhythms of grace. I won't lay anything heavy or ill-fitting on you. Keep company with me and you'll learn to live freely and lightly."

Matthew 11:30, MSG

MAPPING OUT
YOUR RHYTHMS

Rhythms of intentionality help us put God at the center of our lives and seek his calling. God is the Creator, an artist; he will show you what he has called you to put your hands to. Ask the Lord what he has called you to in this season.

Lord, who are you calling me to be?

_____

_____

_____

_____

Lord, what season am I in?

_____

_____

_____

_____

_____

_____

_____

_____

_____

_____

_____

_____

_____

_____

_____

_____

Lord, what daily, weekly, monthly, quarterly, and annual rhythms do you have for me?

_____

_____

_____

_____

_____

_____

_____

_____

_____

_____

_____

_____

_____

_____

_____

_____

PRACTICES

Take a few minutes to review what you wrote about
practices in each sphere in the previous journaling
sections. What stands out? What resonates with you?
What does and doesn't feel like the right fit for you and
your family? Don't worry about creating a detailed plan
just yet. For now, we're simply creating a vision for what
we want these rhythms of intentionality to look like.

PRACTICES OF PRAYER

Daily

_____

_____

_____

_____

_____

_____

_____

_____

_____

Weekly

_____

_____

_____

_____

_____

_____

_____

_____

_____

_____

Monthly

_____

_____

_____

_____

_____

_____

_____

_____

_____

_____

_____

Quarterly

_____

_____

_____

_____

_____

_____

_____

_____

_____

_____

_____

PRACTICES OF REST

Sabbath

_____

_____

_____

_____

_____

_____

_____

_____

_____

Sleep

_____

_____

_____

_____

_____

_____

_____

_____

_____

_____

_____

Seasons

_____

_____

_____

_____

_____

_____

_____

_____

_____

_____

_____

_____

PRACTICES OF RENEWAL

Daily

_____

_____

_____

_____

_____

_____

_____

_____

_____

Weekly

_____

_____

_____

_____

_____

_____

_____

_____

_____

_____

_____

Monthly

_____

_____

_____

_____

_____

_____

_____

_____

_____

_____

_____

Quarterly

_____

_____

_____

_____

_____

_____

_____

Annually

_____

_____

_____

_____

_____

_____

_____

PRACTICES OF RELATIONSHIP

Daily

_____

_____

_____

_____

_____

_____

_____

_____

_____

_____

Weekly

_____

_____

_____

_____

_____

THE INTENTIONAL YEAR JOURNAL

_____

_____

_____

_____

_____

_____

_____

Monthly

_____

_____

_____

_____

_____

_____

_____

_____

_____

_____

_____

_____

Quarterly

_____

_____

_____

_____

_____

_____

_____

Annually

_____

_____

_____

_____

_____

_____

_____

PRACTICES OF WORK

Daily

_____

_____

_____

_____

_____

_____

_____

_____

Weekly

_____

_____

_____

_____

_____

_____

_____

_____

_____

_____

Monthly

_____

_____

_____

_____

_____

_____

_____

_____

_____

_____

_____

Quarterly

_____

_____

_____

_____

_____

_____

_____

_____

_____

_____

Annually

_____

_____

_____

_____

Having a plan doesn't mean you're stuck;

it just means you're being proactive.[10]

SETTING YOUR CALENDAR

Use this space to map out what you want to put on your calendar. Start with your annual rhythms, move into your monthly rhythms, and end with your weekly and daily rhythms. Once you have the vision written out, put it on your calendar!

ANNUAL

_____

_____

_____

_____

_____

_____

_____

_____

_____

QUARTERLY

_____

_____

_____

_____

_____

_____

_____

_____

_____

MONTHLY

January

_____

_____

_____

_____

_____

_____

_____

February

_____

_____

_____

_____

_____

_____

_____

March

_____

_____

_____

_____

_____

_____

_____

April

_____

_____

_____

_____

_____

_____

_____

May

June

July

_____

_____

_____

_____

_____

_____

_____

August

_____

_____

_____

_____

_____

_____

_____

September

_____

_____

_____

_____

_____

_____

_____

October

_____

_____

_____

_____

_____

_____

_____

November

_____

_____

_____

_____

_____

_____

_____

December

_____

_____

_____

_____

_____

_____

_____

_____

WEEKLY

_____

_____

_____

_____

_____

_____

_____

DAILY

Sunday

_____

_____

_____

_____

_____

_____

Monday

_____

_____

_____

_____

_____

_____

_____

Tuesday

_____

_____

_____

_____

_____

_____

_____

Wednesday

_____

_____

_____

_____

_____

_____

_____

Thursday

_____

_____

_____

_____

_____

_____

_____

Friday

_____

_____

_____

_____

_____

_____

_____

_____

Saturday

_____

_____

_____

_____

_____

_____

_____

_____

_____

_____

When we craft a specific plan and write it down,
we're actually embodying our values.[11]

NOTES

1. *The Book of Common Prayer*, 1979 ed. (New York: Oxford University Press, 2005), 454.
2. Holly and Glenn Packiam, *The Intentional Year: Simple Rhythms for Finding Freedom, Peace, and Purpose* (Colorado Springs: NavPress, 2022), 42.
3. *The Intentional Year*, 61.
4. *The Intentional Year*, 79–80.
5. *The Intentional Year*, 95.
6. *The Intentional Year*, 111.
7. *The Intentional Year*, 132.
8. *The Book of Common Prayer*, 261.
9. *The Intentional Year*, 135.
10. *The Intentional Year*, 154.
11. *The Intentional Year*, 184.

YOUR GUIDE TO LIVING WITH FREEDOM, PEACE, AND PURPOSE

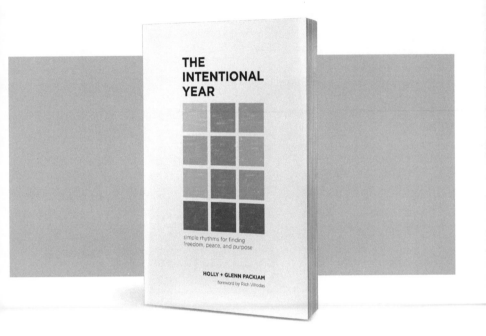

Are you ready to stop living reactively and feeling emotionally exhausted and instead experience the freedom to invest time and energy in the people you value most? *The Intentional Year* is your guide to live into the purpose you were made for. With stories, practices, and a road map to intentionality, Holly and Glenn Packiam will guide you into the simple, sustainable, life-giving rhythms of an intentional life.

Use together with *The Intentional Year Journal*.

Available at NavPress.com or wherever books are sold.